This Big Cat
and Other Cats I've Known

This Big Cat
and Other Cats I've Known

By Beatrice Schenk de Regniers
Illustrated by Alan Daniel

Crown Publishers, Inc.
New York

This Big Cat
and Other Cats I've Known

By Beatrice Schenk de Regniers
Illustrated by Alan Daniel

Crown Publishers, Inc.
New York

Library of Congress Cataloging in Publication Data
De Regniers, Beatrice Schenk.
This big cat, and other cats I've known.
Summary: Describes in rhyme the activities of
cats and the joys of knowing them.
1. Cats—Juvenile poetry. 2. Children's poetry,
American. [1. Cats—Poetry. 2. American poetry]
I. Title.
PS3554.E1155T5   1985   811'.54   84-21498
ISBN 0-517-55538-7
10 9 8 7 6 5 4 3 2 1
First Edition

DEDICATION

To grocery-store cats
delicatessen cats
restaurant cats
and cats in bureau drawers

to country cats
dreaming in sunny meadows

to city cats
sleeping through rainy nights
under parked cars

to long-haired cats
short-haired cats
and cats who shed their hairs
on the living room sofa

to green-eyed cats
blue-eyed cats
cross-eyed cats
and cats with only one eye

to black white orange purple gray beige
and mysterious-moonlight-colored cats

to striped cats
checkered cats
polka-dotted cats
and cats wearing long brown gloves
or short white mittens

to New York cats
California cats
Mexican cats
Parisian cats
Roman cats
Chicago cats
Canadian cats

Crawfordsville cats

Cats, if any, at the North Pole   to all cats everywhere and...

to every boy, girl, or grownup who doesn't
absolutely hate cats
this book (about cats)
is dedicated.

TOO MANY CATS

Cats cats

Too many cats
Cats in bureau drawers
Cats in hats

Cats among the teacups
Cats in bed
I *think* there's a cat
Sitting on my head.

I *know* there's a cat
Sitting on my chair.
Any place you can think of,
You'll find a cat there.

If there's any place that's in or under,
That's where you'll find a cat, by thunder.
For any place that's under or in,
No cat's too fat, no cat's too thin.

This is what I mean...

THIS BIG CAT

This big cat
when small
a shoebox was
his favorite place
of all.

Now
he's old and big and fat.
But no one's ever told him
that
he can no longer fit
inside of it
and so he tries.

He gets his
head
and two big paws
inside
purrs
closes his eyes
and dreams.

It
seems
to
him
he hasn't changed at all.

CATS LOVE BOOKS

Whenever you're sitting and reading a book,
Cat comes over and takes a look.
Then if he likes it, he'll quietly creep on it
And snuggle down and go to sleep on it.

And when the day is dark and damp,
Pussycat suns herself under a lamp.

CAT MYSTERY

The cat that's inside
wants to be outside.

Outside,
the cat wants in.

Wherever the cat is
is where it doesn't want to be.

No one knows
what the cat really wants.

Not even the cat.

SMART CAT

I gave my cat a catnip mouse,
And—can you believe it—
It took him only half a day
To teach me to retrieve it!

CATS KNOW WHAT'S GOOD

Wherever there's sun a cat is sunning.
Where there's a mouse a cat is mousing.
Where there is cream a cat is lapping.
Where there's a lap a cat is purring.

EARLY BREAKFAST

When this cat wants breakfast
you can bet it
knows exactly how to get it—
early.

First
it tries to wake me up
politely.
It jumps onto my bed
and pats my head
three times,
very
lightly.

Then
it sits on my chest
and looks at my toes
while its tail
very
slightly
tickles my nose.
I wake up laughing
and sneezing
and say,
"I'll eat *you* for breakfast
if you don't go
away!"

But the cat
knows I'm teasing.
It purrs in my ear.
It pats my head.
And very soon
I'm out of bed,
giving the cat its breakfast—
early.

CATS ARE GOOD FOR SOMETHING

What are pussycats good for?
What are pussycats good for?

They can wash each other's faces

And help you tie shoelaces

And stretch your papa's braces
and, my dear...

If you're sad and feeling tearful
Then a cat is very cheerful
While it purrs a furry earful
in your ear.

Cats are good for cleaning dishes
Or for sampling sundry fishes
(If they purr, then it's delishes)
So
don't let anyone tell you cats are good for nothing.

THREE FURRY CATS

On a winter's night
I feel just right
with three cats in bed.
I'm warm and snug—
   a cat at my head,
   a cat at my feet,
   a cat I can hug
   in my arms
on a cold winter's night.

On a summer's night
I am too polite
to complain.
Besides, it's impossible
to explain
to
   the cat at my head,
   the cat at my feet,
   the cat in my arms,
that their furry presence
is much too warm
on a hot summer's night!

LOOKS ARE DECEIVING

A cat's tongue
LOOKS
like a rose petal,
while
a cat's tongue
FEELS
like a scratchy
steel
file.

CAT'S WHISKERS

A cat has prickly whiskers
That tickle when he whispers
Cat secrets in your ear.

ABOUT CLAWS AND SCRATCHING

Every cat has 4 soft paws
Every paw has 5 sharp claws.
Every claw likes to latch
Onto something it can scratch.

This is how a cat is sure
To get a proper manicure.

Hmmm. Did I make a mistake when I counted claws?
Count your cat's claws and let me know!

THIS MOTHER CAT

This mother cat
is a worrier.

She worries that
her littlest kit
will fall
out of the basket—

and someone may
step on it.

She worries that
her liveliest kit
will wander away
and never come back.

She worries that
her skinniest kit
is not getting enough milk.

She worries that
maybe her fattest kitten
is eating too much.

She worries that
she can never keep her kittens
clean and neat enough.
She holds each one down
with her big paw
while she gives it
a good tongue-scrubbing.
And when she has finished scrubbing
the last kit,
she begins all over
with the first one.

She worries that
you touch her precious kittens

and fondle them
too much.

Or not enough.

She worries that
you do not know
these kittens
are
    special,
    unique,
    remarkably intelligent,
    and assuredly the
    most adorable creatures
ever to grace the world—
not to mention
the house that happens to shelter them.

We know
that many mothers
are worriers.
But this mother cat
is worrier
(and furrier)
than most
mothers
we know.

POEM BY A CAT

    Purr

purr purr purr purr purrrrr
purr purr purr purr purrrrr
    purr
         purr
purr purr purr
purr purr purr purr purr
pu
  rr
   r

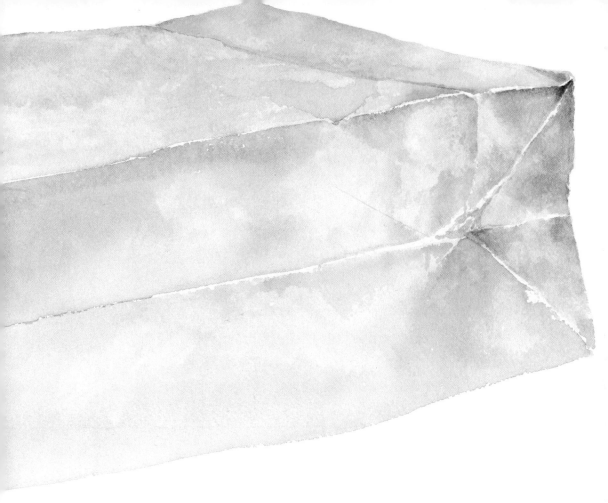

POEM ABOUT A SPECIAL CAT

My cat died.
I cried
      and cried
           and cried
               and cried…

SOME THINGS I KNOW ABOUT CATS

Some cats like milk.
Some don't.
Some cats don't like doughnuts.
Some do.
No two cats are alike.
No one cat is the same always.

If you like surprises
And you are a gentle speaker
And a patient waiter for cats to come to you,
And if you know
NEVER to pet a cat while it is eating
then
probably
cats are for you.

A
SPECIAL
DICTIONARY
TO HELP YOU
UNDERSTAND
CATS

When a cat has its tail
straight up in the air
like this, it is happy.

If a cat fluffs out its fur
so that its tail looks like
a plume, it means the cat is
on the warpath. Usually the
enemy is a catnip mouse
or a piece of string.

A cat is really angry when it flattens its ears back
like this. It may even make an angry hissing noise.
Usually it is another cat who has made the cat so angry.

A cat shakes its paw to show it is disgusted.
If the cat wants cream, and you give it milk,
the cat will shake a paw at the milk and walk away.
Sometimes a cat gets disgusted with you
and shakes a paw at you and walks out of the
room. A cat can shake a front paw or a hind paw.
When it is thoroughly disgusted and fed up,
it shakes all four paws, one after the other.

When a cat shines your shoes like this, it is showing that it likes you and respects you.